# INSTANT ART
## for
# SUNDAY SCHOOLS

**Leah Boyd Barrett**
**Roy Mitchell**
**Susan Sayers**

edited by
**Judy Smith**

# Palm Tree Press

## Acknowledgements

We would like to thank Helen Thacker, Janet Russell and Brian Eden for their helpful comments on this book during the course of its preparation.

## Contributors

*Themes:* Eyes & Ears, Food & Drink, Water & Fire, Hands, and Feet are by Susan Sayers and Roy Mitchell.
Light & Darkness, Times & Seasons, Family & Friends, and The Way are by Leah Boyd Barrett.

*Word Puzzles:* The Word Maze, What Kind of Word, Word Fit and Word Circle puzzles are by Jill Kelbrick.

First published in Great Britain in 1987 by
PALM TREE PRESS
Rattlesden,
Bury St Edmunds, Suffolk IP30 0SZ

ISBN 0 86208 088 6

© 1987 Palm Tree Press
  *(See note about copyright in Introduction)*

Cover design by Roy Mitchell

Typesetting by David Holland Graphics, Colchester
Printed and bound in Great Britain by
The Five Castles Press Limited, Ipswich, Suffolk

# Introduction

Although the main aim of this book is to help Sunday School teachers in the preparation of handouts/worksheets for use with their classes, it will also be an additional resource for people running Holiday Bible Clubs and similar projects. The technique is simple: just choose what you want, cut it out and paste it down with any other text or illustrations you wish to use.

The nine themes into which the material is grouped are simply suggested headings; any individual item can be used in whatever way you choose. The combination of things to do, puzzles etc. is entirely up to you. We hope that this will enable you to make the best possible use of the material the book contains.

## ● cut out/photocopy

The pages have been printed on one side only so that you can cut out what you want without wasting material, and to give the best possible quality of copy for reproduction. As an alternative to cutting out what you require, you could, of course, use photocopies: the book's format allows it to be placed flat on the photocopier.

## ● reduce/enlarge

If you have access to a photocopier which will reduce and enlarge copy you will find it easy to reproduce items from this book in exactly the size you want. However, on the grounds that not everyone has easy access to a machine with this facility, as far as possible we have printed items on which children will write or colour in a size that will enable them to do so easily.

## ● delete/amend

If an item does not quite suit your needs, remember that you can simply 'white-out' unwanted portions with type-correcting fluid, or cut them out.

## ● word puzzles

We have printed the solutions to quizzes and puzzles alongside; however, you may wish to print them upside down or on another page (or to keep them to yourself!).

## ● Bible editions

Different editions of the Bible have been used for the various puzzles and quizzes. To save any possible confusion among children using their own Bibles, you may find it helpful to check them first against the version you use.

## ● make a badge

A number of themes include designs for badges to make; the instructions appear only twice – on the first page of *The Way* and page 5 of *Light and Darkness*. You can, of course, repeat the instructions as many times as you need, by using photocopies.

## ● copyright

Material in this book is copyright-free, provided that it is used for the purpose for which the book is intended. The usual copyright restrictions apply to any use for *commercial* purposes.

## Users' Responses

Although this is the third book in our *Instant Art* series, it is the first one specifically for use with children. As such, it is somewhat experimental in approach, and although we have sought opinions and advice during its preparation, we would welcome your comments. Also, any suggestions you might have for a possible future edition would be warmly received.

# EYES AND EARS 1

## WHICH VOICES COME FROM GOD? WHICH DON'T?

(SHUFFLE THE LETTERS TO FIND THE CENTRE OF BOTH WAYS OF LIVING)

THE MESSAGE MOSES TOOK TO PHARAOH

Use the code to find out what he wanted Pharaoh to do....

(Answer: Let my people go.)

### WHO LISTENED TO GOD?

1. — Genesis 6:13-14 — when God told him to build a boat?
2. — Genesis 12:1 — when God told him to leave his City of Ur?
3. — Exodus 6:10 — when God told him to ask Pharaoh to let the people go from Egypt?
4. — 1 Samuel 16:11-13 — when God told him to choose a young shepherd as a future king?
5. — Luke 1:30-33 — when God told her she would have a son who would save the world?

A. MOSES   B. SAMUEL   C. MARY   D. NOAH   E. ABRAM

Colour in the dotted spaces and find an important message from Jesus (it's in Matthew 7:7)

For instructions for Word Maze puzzles see page 2 of *Hands*.

## EARS    WORD MAZE

The healing of a deaf and dumb man.   (Mark 7:31-35)

Then Jesus left Tyre and Sidon and went down to the Sea of Galilee. Some people brought a man to him who was deaf and could hardly talk, and they begged him to place his hand on the man.

Jesus took the man away from the crowd, and put his fingers in the man's ears. Then he spat and touched the man's tongue, and with a deep sigh said to him "Ephphatha" which was "Be opened." At this the man could hear again and he began to speak plainly.

| T | H | S | R | E | G | N | I | F |
|---|---|---|---|---|---|---|---|---|
| O | A | X | Q | K | A | E | P | S |
| N | N | Z | L | D | E | S | R | P |
| G | D | A | W | L | I | A | E | J |
| U | T | O | I | D | E | Y | R | E |
| E | R | L | O | H | F | G | Y | S |
| C | A | N | F | A | E | D | T | U |
| G | D | E | H | C | U | O | T | S |
| B | E | O | P | E | N | E | D | Y |

### Solution

JESUS
TYRE
SIDON
GALILEE
DEAF
TALK
HAND
CROWD
FINGERS
EARS
TOUCHED
TONGUE
BE OPENED
HEAR
SPEAK

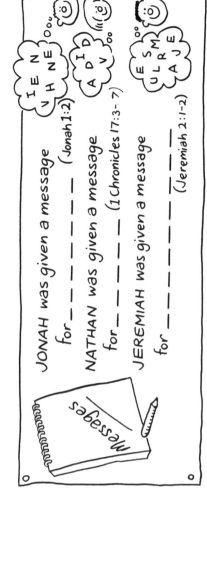

JONAH was given a message for – – – – – –    (Jonah 1:2)

NATHAN was given a message for – – – – –    (1 Chronicles 17:3-7)

JEREMIAH was given a message for – – – – – – – – –    (Jeremiah 2:1-2)

Messages

**(Answers:** Nineveh, David, Jerusalem)

READ MATTHEW 7:1-5

YOU'VE GOT A SPECK IN YOUR EYE – THAT WON'T DO, YOU KNOW!

HE'S GOT A BIG PLANK IN HIS!

Moses and the people of Israel were led through the desert day and night...

A pillar of – – – – by day,    a pillar of – – – – by night

(Read Exodus 13:17-22)

YOU CAN'T WEAR THOSE OLD JEANS TO CHURCH!

BUT YOU'RE WEARING OLD CLOTHES!

YES, BUT I'M NOT GOING TO CHURCH – I'M TOO BUSY

## WORD FIT

### EYES AND EARS

1 across — John 9:1-7
When Jesus healed the blind man which pool was the man told to wash in (6)

2 across — Mark 7:31-32
What was the name of the region where Jesus healed the deaf man (9)

3 across — Acts 9:3-4
Who heard a voice on the way to Damascus (4)

6 across — 1 Samuel 3:2
Whose sight was failing (3)

4 down — Matthew 17:3
and 6 down At the Transfiguration who did the disciples see talking to Jesus (5 & 6)

5 down — Mark 10:46-52
What was the name of the blind beggar who received his sight back (10)

### Solution

| | | |
|---|---|---|
| Across | 1. | Siloam |
| | 2. | Decapolis |
| | 3. | Saul |
| | 6. | Eli |
| Down | 4. | Moses |
| | 5. | Bartimaeus |
| | 6. | Elijah |

## THINGS AREN'T ALWAYS WHAT THEY SEEM!

1. Are these lines straight or bent?

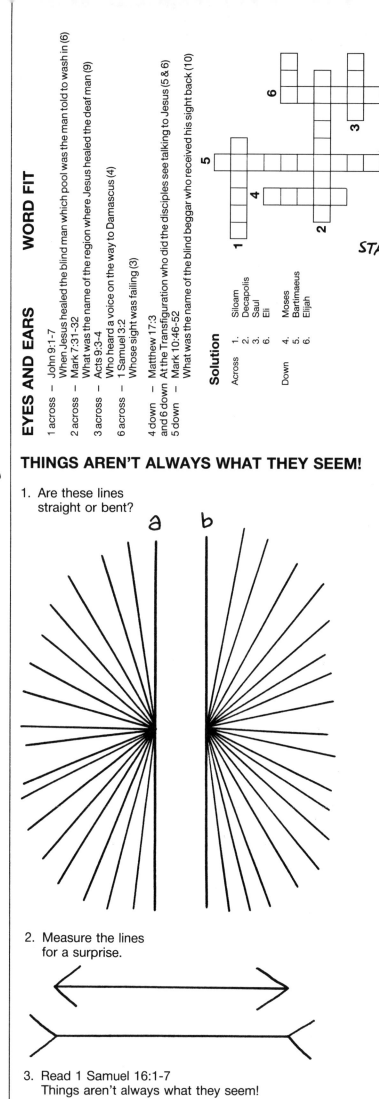

2. Measure the lines for a surprise.

3. Read 1 Samuel 16:1-7
Things aren't always what they seem!

## Find your way to the centre of the ear, reading Jesus' message as you go....

START

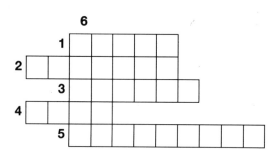

WORDS OF COMFORT...

## WHO HEARD . . .?

### Clues

*Across*
1. Who heard that his 'dead' son was alive after all? (Genesis 45:25-26)
2. Who heard the rattle of bones? (Ezekiel 37:7)
3. Who heard God calling him when he was a boy? (1 Samuel 3:2-4)
4. Who heard he would have to escape in a basket let down a city wall? (Acts 9:23-25)
5. Who heard angels singing? (Luke 2:13-15)

*Down*
6. Who hears us whenever we pray?

### Solution

1. Jacob
2. Ezekiel
3. Samuel
4. Saul
5. Shepherds
6. Jesus

JOIN the DOTS...
for something Jacob
saw in a dream...

(GENESIS 28 : 10-12)

zzzzz

'Speak; your servant is listening.'

READ THE STORY IN 1 SAMUEL 3

SAMUEL, SAMUEL

...then fill in what Samuel replied

What's that word again?

YOU'RE RIGHT!

Look at it in a mirror and smile...!!
Try using it more today!!

## CAN YOU FIND –

a book
a torch
a map

## in the picture?

Not another album!
All the money you waste!
You ought not to be so greedy!

You've got bananas in your ears

PARDON?

You've GOT BANANAS IN YOUR EARS!

EH?

You've GOT BANANAS IN YOUR EARS!!!

I CAN'T HEAR YOU — I'VE GOT BANANAS IN MY EARS!

## EYES AND EARS

## WHAT KIND OF WORD

WHICH EYE IS:

1.  EYE – – – –        – a cup to bathe the eyes
2.  EYE – – – – – –    – a row of hairs on the eyelids
3.  EYE – – –          – something that is ugly to look at
4.  EYE – – – – – –    – a person who sees a crime committed

### Solution

1. EYEBATH
2. EYELASHES
3. EYESORE
4. EYEWITNESS

BUILD the PYRAMID to find the message....

CHRIST
ON
BUILD
JESUS
YOUR
LIFE

Help the shepherd search for his lost sheep.....

BAAA!

Read 'The Parable of the Lost Sheep' in Matthew 18:10-14 or Luke 15:3-7.

COLOUR IT IN

JESUS ONCE HEALED A MAN WHO WAS DEAF AND WHO COULDN'T SPEAK PROPERLY (THE WHOLE STORY IS IN MARK 7: 32-35) FINISH THE WALL WITH THE RIGHT BRICKS TO FIND OUT HOW JESUS HEALED HIM

Jesus put his ___ in the man's ___ and he ___ on his ___ Then he ___ ' ___ ' which means 'Be ___ ' The man found he could hear and speak.

fingers   ears   'Ephphatha!'   tongue
sighed   opened   spat

# LIGHT AND DARKNESS 1

## ~ Make a Lantern ~

scissors

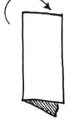

and glue.

To make a lantern you need:

21 cm

30 cm

Coloured paper or card

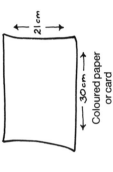

1. Cut a strip for the handle off one narrow end.

2. Fold the paper in half lengthways.

3. Draw a pencil line about 2 cm. from one long edge.

4. Cut along folded edge to pencil line.

glue on handle

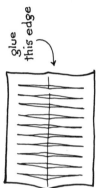

glue this edge

5. Open out lantern and glue one short edge.

6. Stick it to the opposite edge and glue on the strip for the handle.

---

## IN THE BEGINNING...

there was DARKNESS

and then God made
~ LIGHT ~

Phew!

L.B.B.

Genesis 1:1-5

---

## unJuMBLe the words
and match them to the pictures.

1. d e c n l a  <u>        </u>

2. e l f a r  <u>        </u>

3. p l m a  <u>        </u>

4. t a e l r n n  <u>          </u>

5. o h t r c  <u>       </u>

Can you think of any other kinds of LIGHT?

## LIGHT

**WHAT KIND OF WORD**

WHICH LIGHT IS:

1. LIGHT – – – – –    – a building near the sea to warn ships of danger
2. LIGHT – – – – – –   – not very heavy
3. LIGHT – – – –     – a ball of glass used in an electric light
4. LIGHT – – – – – – – –  – given to thieving and robbing

### Solution

1. LIGHTHOUSE
2. LIGHTWEIGHT
3. LIGHT BULB
4. LIGHT-FINGERED

## LIGHT AND DARKNESS

### WORD CIRCLE

How many words of three letters or more can you make from the letters in the circle? When you have found as many as you can, try and make one word of seven letters using all the letters. This word has something to do with light.

(Word circle contains letters: M, D, T, E, A, Y, I)

AID
AIM
ATE
DAM
DAME
DATE
DAY
DIM
DIME
DYE
EAT
EDIT
MAD
MADE
MAT
MATE
MAY
MET
MITE
TAME
TEA
TEAM
TIDE
TIDY
TIME

DAYTIME

Circle the things you can do with your eyes closed.

## ~Make a Spectrum Wheel~

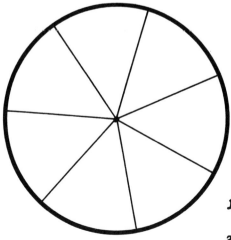

When you look at a rainbow, you are seeing light split up into the 7 colours of the spectrum. To make a spectrum wheel, you will need:
- colours (violet, indigo, blue, green, yellow, orange and red)
- scissors
- string about 25cm long

1. Trace the wheel onto thin white card and cut out.
2. Colour triangles the colours of the spectrum.
3. Make a hole in the centre and pass the string through.
4. Spin the wheel holding both ends of the string. Then pull the ends taut. What happens to all the colours?

Darkness: The Ninth Plague of Egypt
(Exodus 10:21-29)

## ~ Fairy Lights ~

Can you think of 10 "good turns"?
Colour a fairy light for every good
turn you can think of.
(Colour the star for free!)

1. _____
2. _____
3. _____
4. _____
5. _____
6. _____
7. _____
8. _____
9. _____
10. _____

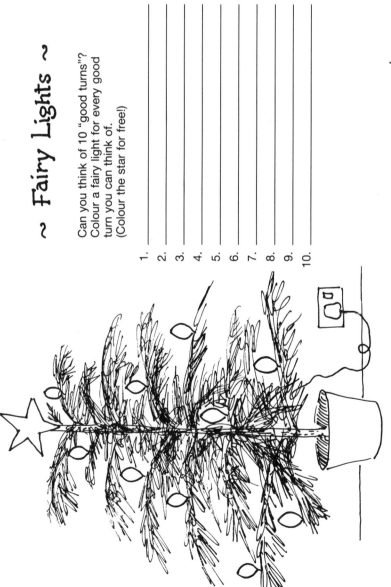

Colour the dotted spaces yellow to light
Arthur's way through the tunnel.
Colour the other spaces black, purple
and grey.

# LIGHT AND DARKNESS 4

## ~ The Transfiguration ~

1. Who went up the mountain with Jesus?

2. "Jesus' face shone like the sun and his clothes became as dazzling as . . ."

3. Who else appeared to the disciples?

4. A voice from the cloud said: "this is my son, the Beloved; he enjoys my favour. – – – – – – to him."

5. Jesus said to the disciples:

## DARKNESS    WORD MAZE

The Crucifixion.   (Matthew 27:32-54)

After Pontius Pilate had condemned Jesus to death, three crosses were set up at a place called Golgotha. The soldiers fixed Jesus to the cross with nails, and on the other crosses were two thieves who jeered at him.

Jesus had been hanging on the cross in the sun all the morning, and at mid-day darkness came over the whole land and lasted for three hours. In the middle of the afternoon Jesus gave a loud cry and died. The earth shook as though there had been an earthquake and the centurion who was guarding Jesus said "Surely this man was the Son of God."

For instructions for Word Maze puzzles see page 2 of *Hands*.

| S | S | E | N | K | R | A | D | N |
|---|---|---|---|---|---|---|---|---|
| A | D | O | G | F | O | N | O | S |
| S | H | O | O | K | Z | I | H | T |
| S | U | T | S | Q | R | C | T | H |
| O | Q | I | O | U | B | R | R | I |
| R | G | C | T | G | S | Y | A | E |
| C | V | N | P | N | L | E | E | V |
| D | E | A | T | H | O | O | J | E |
| C | E | T | A | L | I | P | G | S |

## SOLUTION

| S | S | E | N | K | R | A | D | N |
|---|---|---|---|---|---|---|---|---|
| A | D | O | G | F | O | N | O | S |
| S | H | O | O | K | Z | I | H | T |
| S | U | T | S | Q | R | C | T | H |
| O | Q | I | O | U | B | R | R | I |
| R | G | C | T | G | S | Y | A | E |
| C | V | N | P | N | L | E | E | V |
| D | E | A | T | H | O | O | J | E |
| C | E | T | A | L | I | R | G | S |

PONTIUS
PILATE
JESUS
DEATH
GOLGOTHA
CROSS
THIEVES
DARKNESS
CRY
EARTH
SHOOK
CENTURION
SON OF GOD

## Sort these words into the right boxes:- (you can add your own)

Brightness    Night    Joy

Happiness    Blindness    Glow

Gloom    Frown    Smile

Sight    Clear    Trapped

Life    Day

Hatred    Death    Love

Free    Misery

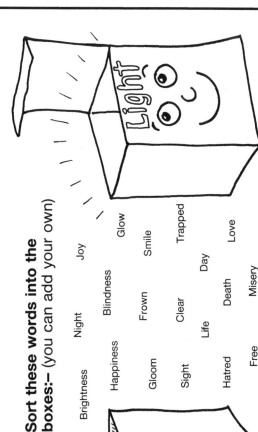

# LIGHT AND DARKNESS 5

DANNY DARK        and        LARRY LIGHT

Who is thinking what?
Complete the cartoon.

Parable of the Lamp (Luke 8:16-18)

## LIGHT AND DARKNESS

### WORD FIT

1 across – Matthew 17:1-2
  Who did Jesus describe as "a lamp that burned and gave light" (4)

2 across – Matthew 17:1-3
  At the Transfiguration what became as white as the light (7)

3 across – Genesis 1:3-5
and 5 down What did God call the light and the darkness (3 & 5)

4 down – Mark 5:15
  What sort of light does Jesus speak about (4)

5 down – see 3 across

6 down – Exodus 10:21-23
  Which country was covered by darkness for three days (5)

### Solution

| Across | | Down | |
|---|---|---|---|
| 1. | John | 4. | Lamp |
| 2. | Clothes | 5. | Night |
| 3. | Day | 6. | Egypt |

## ~ Badge to make ~

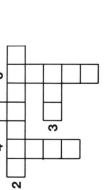
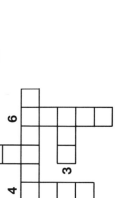

To make this badge you will need:-

- a piece of card about 9 cm x 9 cm
  (you can cut it off an empty cereal box)
- scissors          • sellotape
- glue              • felt tips
- a small safety pin

1. Colour the badge with felt tips.
2. Cut it out and glue it onto card.
3. Cut round the badge.*
4. Sellotape the safety pin onto the back.

*NOTE
badges can be covered with self-adhesive clear
plastic, obtainable from ironmongers.

# FOOD AND DRINK 1

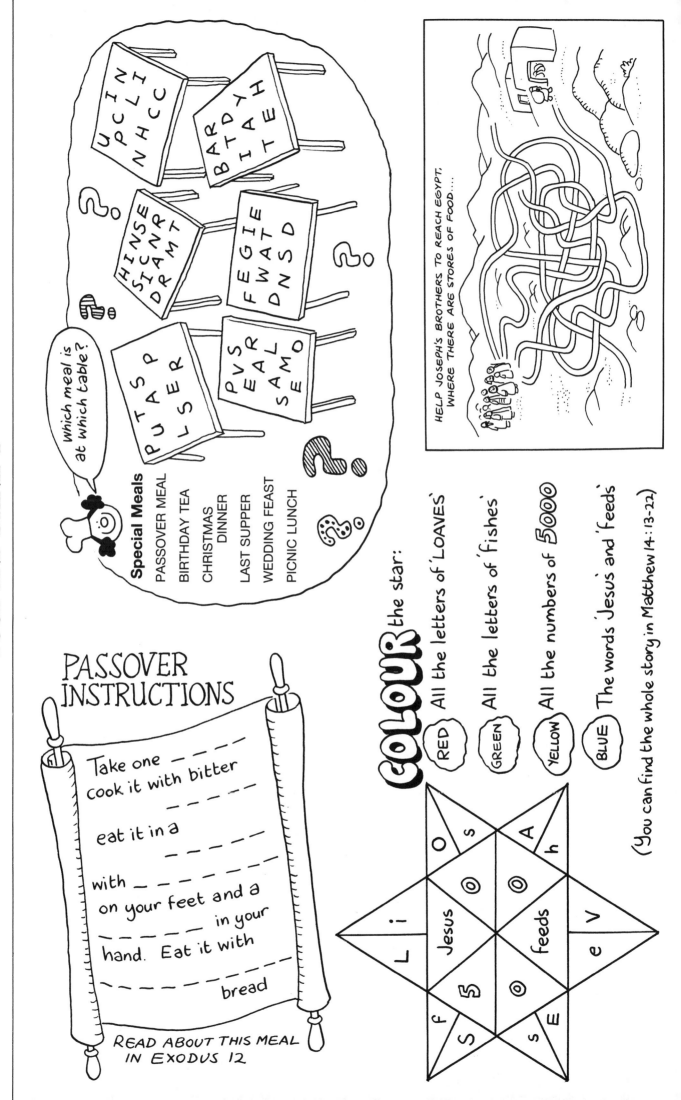

Which meal is at which table?

**Special Meals**

PASSOVER MEAL
BIRTHDAY TEA
CHRISTMAS DINNER
LAST SUPPER
WEDDING FEAST
PICNIC LUNCH

HELP JOSEPH'S BROTHERS TO REACH EGYPT, WHERE THERE ARE STORES OF FOOD....

## PASSOVER INSTRUCTIONS

Take one _ _ _ _
cook it with bitter
_ _ _ _ _
eat it in a _ _ _ _
with _ _ _ _ _
on your feet and a
_ _ _ _ _ in your
hand. Eat it with
_ _ _ _ _ _ _ _ bread

READ ABOUT THIS MEAL IN EXODUS 12

## COLOUR the star:

(RED) All the letters of 'LOAVES'

(GREEN) All the letters of 'fishes'

(YELLOW) All the numbers of 5000

(BLUE) The words 'Jesus' and 'feeds'

(You can find the whole story in Matthew 14: 13-22)

# FOOD AND DRINK 2

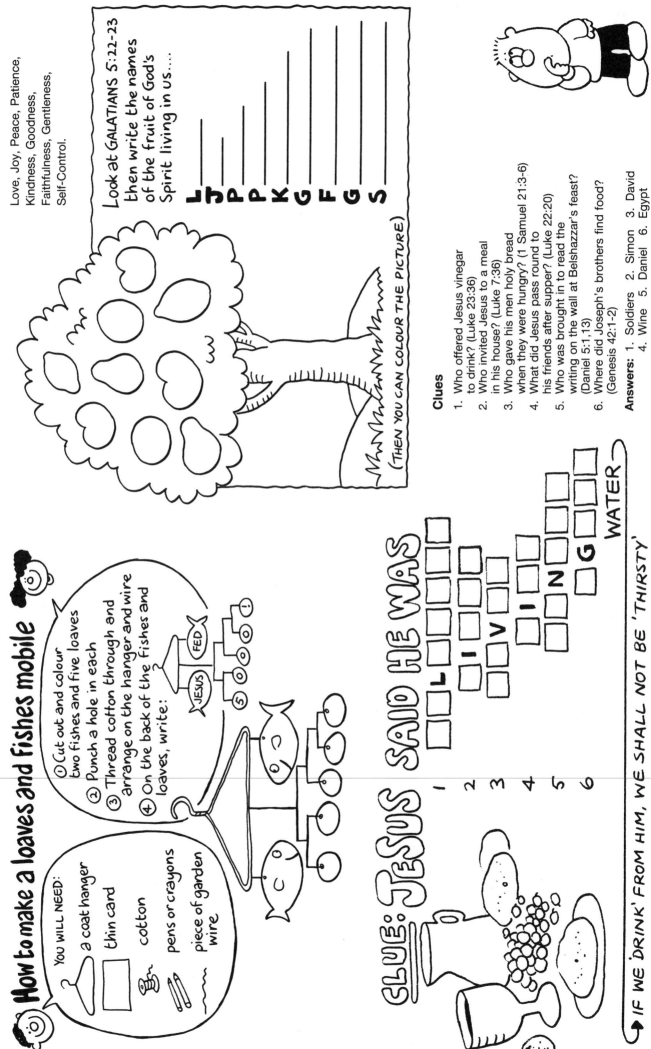

## How to make a loaves and fishes mobile

YOU WILL NEED:

- a coat hanger
- thin card
- cotton
- pens or crayons
- piece of garden wire

① Cut out and colour two fishes and five loaves

② Punch a hole in each

③ Thread cotton through and arrange on the hanger and wire

④ On the back of the fishes and loaves, write:

JESUS   FED   I   5000

Love, Joy, Peace, Patience, Kindness, Goodness, Faithfulness, Gentleness, Self-Control.

Look at GALATIANS 5:22-23 then write the names of the fruit of God's Spirit living in us.....

L
J
P
P
K
G
F
G
S

(THEN YOU CAN COLOUR THE PICTURE)

## CLUE: JESUS SAID HE WAS

1.  (L)
2.  (I)
3.  (V)
4.  (I) (N)
5.  (G)
6.  (WATER)

IF WE 'DRINK' FROM HIM, WE SHALL NOT BE 'THIRSTY'

## Clues

1. Who offered Jesus vinegar to drink? (Luke 23:36)
2. Who invited Jesus to a meal in his house? (Luke 7:36)
3. Who gave his men holy bread when they were hungry? (1 Samuel 21:3-6)
4. What did Jesus pass round to his friends after supper? (Luke 22:20)
5. Who was brought in to read the writing on the wall at Belshazzar's feast? (Daniel 5:1,13)
6. Where did Joseph's brothers find food? (Genesis 42:1-2)

**Answers:** 1. Soldiers  2. Simon  3. David  4. Wine  5. Daniel  6. Egypt

# FOOD AND DRINK 3

## DRINK

### WORD MAZE

The wedding at Cana. (John 2:1-11)

A wedding took place at Cana in Galilee. Jesus and his mother, and the disciples had all been invited to the banquet. When the wine had all gone Jesus told the servants to fill six stone jars with water. And the jars were filled to the brim. When the water was tasted by the master of the banquet, he thought it was the best wine and that it had been saved till last. Only the servants knew that the jars were filled with water and that Jesus had turned it into wine. This was the first miracle of Jesus.

| A | W | S | B | E | N | I | W | M |
|---|---|---|---|---|---|---|---|---|
| T | C | E | T | D | F | G | S | I |
| E | H | A | D | O | K | T | U | R |
| U | M | N | J | D | N | L | S | A |
| Q | O | A | M | A | I | E | E | C |
| N | T | C | V | P | Q | N | J | L |
| A | H | R | S | R | A | J | G | E |
| B | E | R | E | T | A | W | R | S |
| S | R | E | E | L | I | L | A | G |

**Solution**

WEDDING
CANA
GALILEE
JESUS
MOTHER
BANQUET
WINE
SERVANTS
STONE
JARS
WATER
MIRACLE

For instructions for Word Maze puzzles see page 2 of *Hands.*

## CRACK THE CODE...

TO READ THE MESSAGE FROM JESUS *(it's in JOHN 6:48-51)*

here's the 'key'

(**Answer:** I am the bread of life. If anyone eats of this bread he will live for ever.)

Read 1 Chronicles 12:40

## A ROYAL FEAST

WHEN DAVID WAS KING, THERE WAS A GREAT FEAST....

...CAN YOU WORK OUT WHAT GOODIES THERE WERE?

EINW

KCAES of FGIS

NXEO

RINI STSR C TULE SAS E

EHSEP

LIO

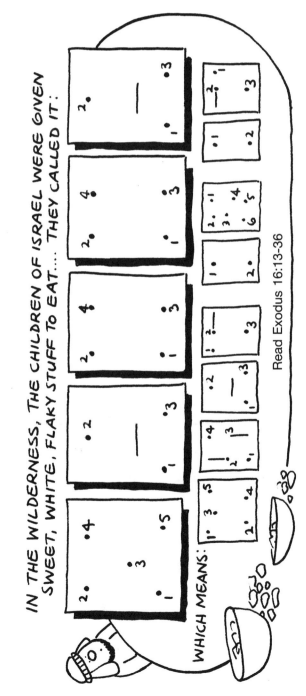

IN THE WILDERNESS, THE CHILDREN OF ISRAEL WERE GIVEN SWEET, WHITE, FLAKY STUFF TO EAT.... THEY CALLED IT:

WHICH MEANS:

Read Exodus 16:13-36

## FOOD AND DRINK      WORD FIT

1 across – Matthew 14:14-21
How many loaves of bread were there when Jesus fed the five thousand (4)
2 across – Ezekiel 25:4
and 4 down Which food and drink is mentioned (4 & 5)
3 across – Luke 6:43-45
Which fruit does Jesus talk about in this parable (6)

4 down – see 2 across
5 down – John 2:1-11
At which family celebration did Jesus turn the water into wine (7)
6 down – Exodus 16:31
What did the people of Israel call the bread that the Lord sent (5)

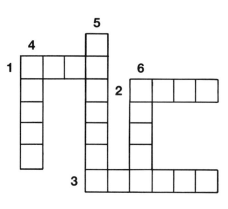

### Solution

Across    1.    Five
          2.    Milk
          3.    Grapes

Down      4.    Fruit
          5.    Wedding
          6.    Manna

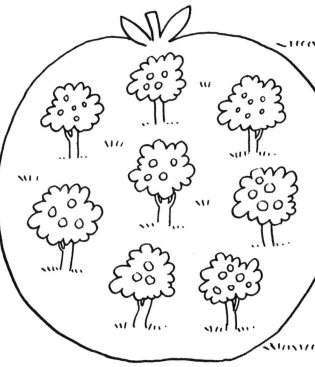

ADAM and EVE were told they could eat the fruit from EVERY TREE BUT ONE (Genesis 2:16-17)

① Circle the one they were told NOT to eat from

② What was it called? The tree of _____

_____

③ What would happen if they did eat its fruit?

_____

## FIND YOUR WAY TO THE PICNIC...

**ON** and **ON** and **ON**...
LABEL THE INGREDIENTS WHICH DIDN'T RUN OUT (1 KINGS 17:10-16)

WHAT WAS BAKED?   WHO ATE IT?

Oil   Flour   Bread   Elijah

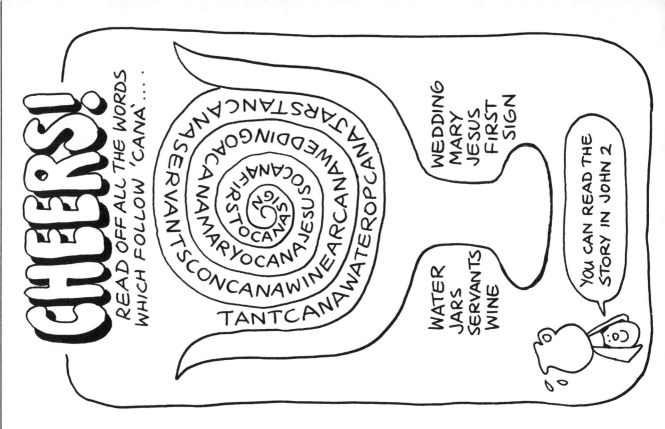

| FOOD | WHAT KIND OF WORD |
|---|---|

**WHICH BREAD IS:**

1. BREAD – – – – – – – a woven container for bread
2. BREAD – – – – – – – a crumbled loaf
3. BREAD – – – – – – – a person who earns a living for a family
4. BREAD – – – – – – a piece of wood on which bread is cut

**Solution**

1. BREADBASKET
2. BREADCRUMBS
3. BREADWINNER
4. BREADBOARD

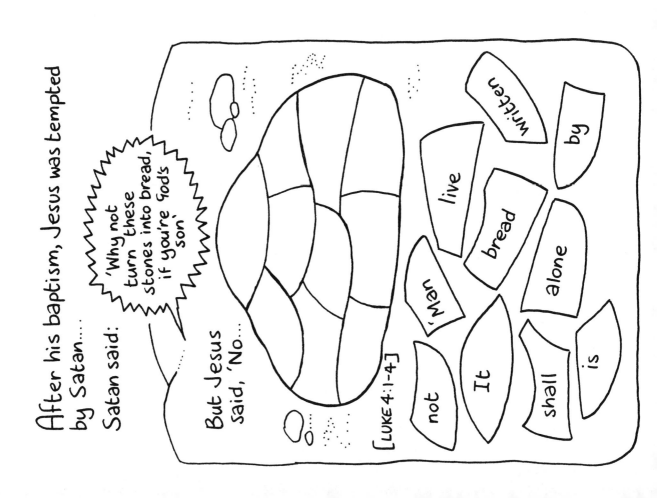

STAY AWAKE

The master is coming home!
Can you stay awake?
You will need a dice, and a
counter for each player.

To find out more, read
Mark 13:33-37.

~ The True Vine ~

Love

Faith

Hope

Peace

Hatred

Envy

Greed

Lies

L.B.B.

This vine needs pruning to keep it growing
at its best.

For instructions on pruning this vine, read
John 15:1-8.

~ Sow 'n Grow ~

A windowsill garden for you to make

**You will need:**
1. margarine tubs
2. soil
3. gravel

**For growing:**
1. mustard & cress seeds
2. dried whole beans, soaked overnight
3. beetroot, carrot or turnip tops,
   shoots trimmed to around 2½ cm
4. "instant" plants, i.e. grass, moss, celery
   tops, pineapple tops
5. any other seeds or small bulbs you fancy
   growing, though they will take longer.

• Fill tubs to 2 cm from rims with soil (gravel for vegetable tops).
• Plant seeds or beans thinly.
• Cover any roots of "instant" plants well.
• Water regularly but do not soak.
• Keep on windowsill or near a sunny window.

## GOD CREATES THE WORLD

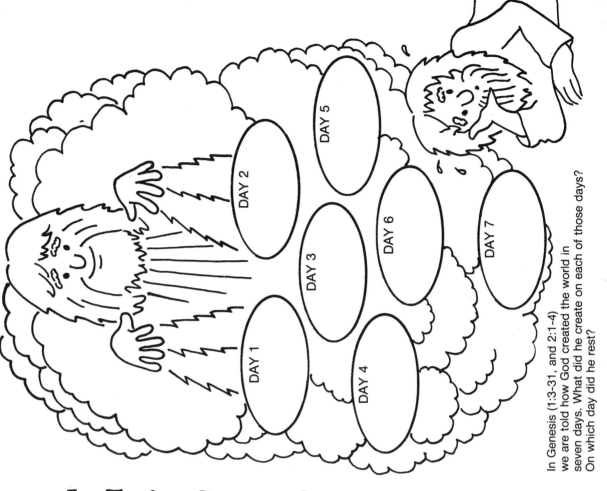

DAY 2
DAY 5
DAY 3
DAY 6
DAY 7
DAY 1
DAY 4

In Genesis (1:3-31, and 2:1-4) we are told how God created the world in seven days. What did he create on each of those days? On which day did he rest?

## ~ An Easter Crossword ~

(The answers are in Matthew 27 & 28)

### Across

1. When Jesus died, the earth shook with one of these.
2. The angel's message was "Jesus has – – – – –."
3. This disciple betrayed Jesus.
4. The governor who handed Jesus over to the people.
5. What the elders gave soldiers to tell lies about Jesus' resurrection.
6. Judas received this many pieces of silver.
7. Jesus' body was wrapped in one of these.
8. Jesus sent word for the disciples to meet him here.
9. What did Pilate wash? (3,4)

### Down

10. The prisoner released in place of Jesus.
11. Jesus was buried for this number of days.
12. The two Marys were greeted by one on the third day.
13. The chief priests and pharisees asked Pilate to put these in front of Jesus's tomb.
14. Jesus was offered this to drink on a sponge.
15. Jesus had a "crown" made of these.
16. The soldiers did this to Jesus before they put him on the cross.
17. This man helped Jesus to carry his cross.
18. Jesus's body was placed in the tomb of Joseph of – – – – – – – – –

### Solution

*Across*
1. Earthquake
2. Risen
3. Judas
4. Pilate
5. Bribe
6. Thirty
7. Shroud
8. Galilee
9. His hands

*Down*
10. Barabbas
11. Three
12. Angel
13. Guards
14. Vinegar
15. Thorns
16. Scourged
17. Simon
18. Arimathaea

## ~ Year-round Carnations ~

You will need:
- white or coloured tissues (2 per flower)
- sellotape
- 50 cm length of green garden wire for each flower.
- an unwanted used lipstick
- left over spray cologne

1. Place 2 tissues one on top of the other, opened out flat.
2. Fold the tissues crosswise in accordion fashion

3. Bend the folded tissues in half and secure the centre with sellotape.

4. Bend the wire in half over the sellotape and twist to form a stem.
5. Carefully tear the very edges of the flower to resemble the petals of a carnation.
6. Open out all the layers of the tissues.
7. Brush with lipstick to tint the edges and spray with cologne.

## TIMES AND SEASONS WORD CIRCLE

How many words of four letters or more can you make from the letters in the circle? No proper names can be used and no plurals. When you have found as many as you can, try and make one word of nine letters using all the letters.

This word is a very special time of year.

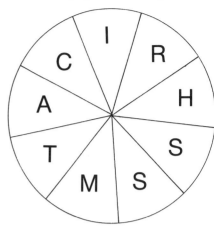

| | |
|---|---|
| CART | HISS |
| CAST | MARSH |
| CHAIR | MASH |
| CHARM | MASS |
| CHART | MAST |
| CHAT | MATCH |
| CRASH | RICH |
| HAIR | SCAR |
| HARM | SHAM |
| HART | SMART |

SMASH
STAIR
STAR
STIR
THIS
TRAM
TRIM

CHRISTMAS

## ~ The Judge & the Widow ~

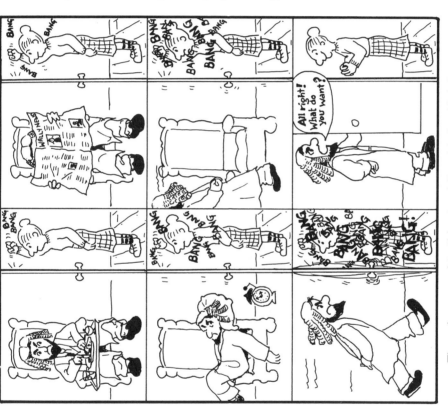

There is a moral to this story! Read Luke 18:1-8 to find out what it is.

Where do we come from?   Where are we going?   Colour the dotted spaces to find out.

# ~ A Year Clock
## for you to make ~

You will need:
– stiff cardboard
– scissors
– glue
– fine felt tips
– a wing clip (split pin)
– 5 cm length of ribbon.

Colour the pictures carefully, then glue the clock and hand onto the cardboard. Cut round the clock. Cut out the month hand and make a hole through the mark and through the centre of the clock. Fix the hand onto the clock with the wing clip. Glue the ends of the ribbon behind 'July' to make a loop for hanging. Now you can enter any of the dates on the list.

Enter these dates in the correct month:

Advent
Christmas
Lent
Easter
Harvest Time
May Day
Summer holidays

Guy Fawkes
All Saints Day
New Year's Day
Birthdays
Anniversaries
Other special
dates

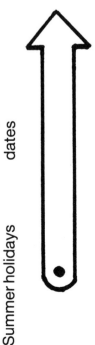

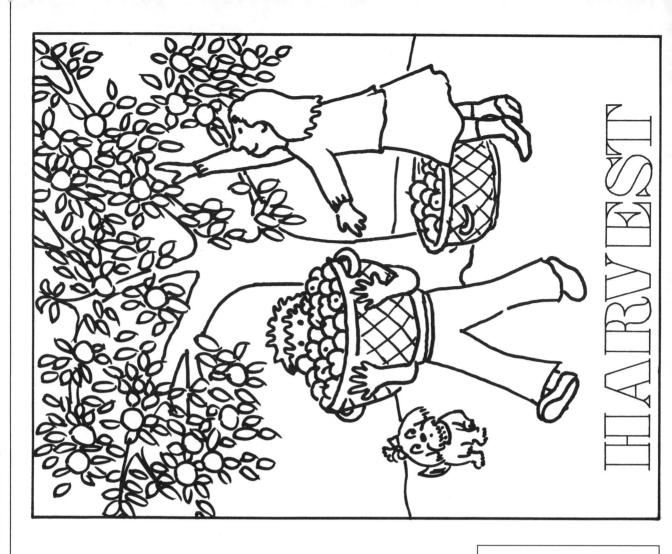

## ~ An Invitation ~

Dear
_____ ,
You are invited to be one of my chosen people. Hope you can come.
Love,
GOD.
R.S.V.P. ✂

Dear God,

☐ I would love to come. Please tell me what I have to do.

☐ Sorry, I'm too busy. Maybe some other time.

Signed: _____

There is a story about some invited guests. Read Luke 14:15-24.

For instructions on how to make a badge see page 5 of *Light & Darkness.*

**Badge to make** ~

For instructions for Word Maze puzzles see page 2 of *Hands.*

## SEASONS   WORD MAZE

Harvest

We plough the fields, and scatter
The good seed on the land,
But it is fed and watered
By God's almighty hand.
He sends the snow in winter
The warmth to swell the grain,
The breezes and the sunshine,
And soft refreshing rain.
All good gifts around us
Are sent from Heaven above,
Then thank the Lord, O thank the Lord
For all his love.

| Z | P | D | E | R | E | T | A | W |
|---|---|---|---|---|---|---|---|---|
| X | K | L | R | B | C | D | E | A |
| B | D | N | O | A | F | N | G | R |
| R | L | R | A | U | I | H | S | M |
| E | O | E | O | H | G | N | T | T |
| E | V | T | S | L | T | H | F | H |
| Z | E | N | S | D | L | E | I | F |
| E | U | I | D | E | E | S | G | J |
| S | K | W | O | N | S | L | B | P |

**Solution**

PLOUGH
FIELDS
SEED
WATERED
SNOW
WINTER
WARMTH
BREEZES
SUNSHINE
RAIN
GIFTS
THANK
LORD
LOVE

| Z | P | D | E | R | E | T | A | W |
|---|---|---|---|---|---|---|---|---|
| X | K | L | R | B | C | D | E | A |
| B | D | N | O | A | F | N | G | R |
| R | L | R | A | U | I | H | S | M |
| E | O | E | O | H | G | N | T | T |
| E | V | T | S | L | T | H | F | H |
| Z | E | N | S | D | L | E | I | F |
| E | U | I | D | E | E | S | G | J |
| S | K | W | O | N | S | L | B | P |

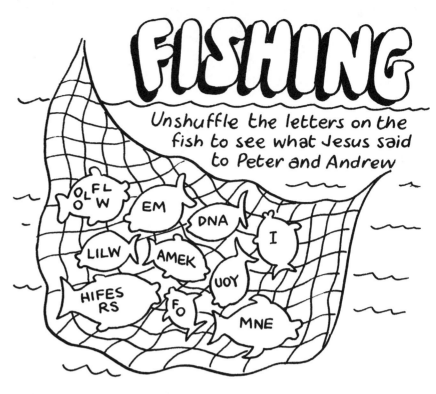

# FISHING

Unshuffle the letters on the fish to see what Jesus said to Peter and Andrew

Matthew 4:18-20; Mark 1:16-20; Luke 5:1-11

(See also the 'What a Catch' puzzle on page 2 of the *Feet* section.)

## MAKE A CANDLE ADVENT CALENDAR

Mark off 24 notches and at the last one stick a gold star. Burn the candle down a notch each day.

Or just mark 4 notches and burn the candle each Sunday of Advent.

## WATER

WHICH WATER IS:

1. WATER – – – –   – a large barrel for rain water
2. WATER – – – – – –   – land which is flooded and cannot be used
3. WATER – – – – – – –   – the sign of the Zodiac, Aquarius
4. WATER – – – – –   – a green plant used in salads

## WHAT KIND OF WORD

### Solution
1. WATERBUTT
2. WATERLOGGED
3. WATERCARRIER
4. WATERCRESS

Shadrach. Meshach. Abednego.

# WHO IS IN THE FIERY FURNACE?

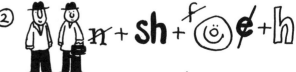

CHECK IF YOU ARE RIGHT IN DANIEL 3

# PUZZLES

## COLOUR IT IN!

## WATER

### WORD CIRCLE

How many words of three letters or more can you make from the letters in the circle? No proper names can be used and no plurals. When you have found as many as you can, try and make one word of seven letters using all the letters. This word has something to do with water.

AIM    PAT
APT    PIT
ASP    SAP
BAIT   SAT
BAP   SIP
BAT   SIT
BIT   STAB
IMP   STAMP
MAP   TAB
MAST  TAP
MAT   TIP
PAST

BAPTISM

(Word circle letters: S, B, I, T, M, P, A)

## a TRICK..

How can you make 9 matches into 10 without adding or breaking any?

ANSWER: TEN

## HELP PETER TO SWIM TO JESUS...

COLOUR IN THE RIGHT ANSWERS
(JOHN 21: 1-14)

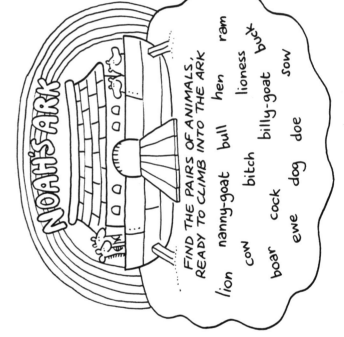

| fish and bread | 99 | fish and rice | 153 | fish and potatoes | 112 |
| | afternoon | dawn | | evening | |
| Red Sea | | Dead Sea | | Sea of Tiberias | |

IT IS THE LORD!

① Which sea were they on?
② What time was it?
③ How many fish did they catch?
④ What did Jesus give them for breakfast?

And this happened AFTER Jesus had been crucified — so it proved that he was

LAVIE GAANI!

## NOAH'S ARK

FIND THE PAIRS OF ANIMALS, READY TO CLIMB INTO THE ARK

lion   bull   hen   ram
nanny-goat   lioness   buck
cow   bitch   billy-goat   sow
boar   cock   doe
ewe   dog

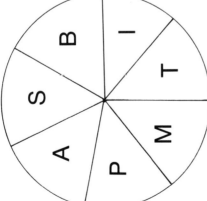
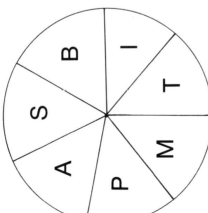
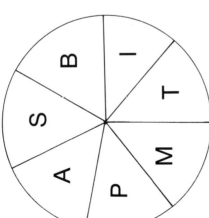

WHAT DO ALL THESE NEED TO SURVIVE?

**Answer:** Whale, Cat, Tree, Pear, Bear – WATER

## WHO WAS THE BABY WHO LED HIS PEOPLE TO FREEDOM WHEN HE GREW UP?

To find his name, fill in the words across.

1. The Egyptians were killing every – – – – Hebrew child.
2. The king of Egypt was called – – – – – – –.
3. The baby boy was hidden among the – – – – – –.
4. He was floating in a – – – – – –.
5. His own mother was asked to – – – – – him.

(The whole story is in Exodus 2.)

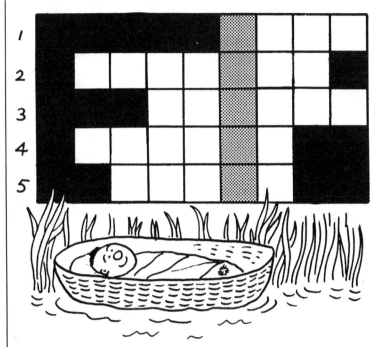

(**Answer:** Jonah)

**Answers:** 1. Male  2. Pharoah  3. Rushes  4. Basket  5. Nurse  (Moses)

CAN YOU CRACK THE CODE TO DISCOVER WHAT MOSES HEARD GOD SAY FROM THE BURNING BUSH?

"Ia mth eGo do fyou rfather sth eGo do fAbraha mth eGo do fIsaa can dth eGo do fJaco b"

The last letter of each word is joined to the next word.

## FIRE AND WATER    WORD FIT

1 across – Daniel 3:1-29
2 across    Who were cast into the fiery furnace by Nebuchadnezzar
and 3 down (8, 7 & 8)

3 down – see 1 across
4 down – Exodus 3:2-3
    Who saw the Lord appear in a burning bush (5)
5 down – Luke 5:1-11
    What was another name for the Sea of Galilee (10)
6 down – Matthew 3:13
    In which river was Jesus baptised by John (6)

### Solution

Across    1.    Abednego
          2.    Meshach

Down      3.    Shadrach
          4.    Moses
          5.    Gennesaret
          6.    Jordan

## WATER

## WORD MAZE

Noah's ark.   (Genesis 6,7,8 & 9)

God had been saddened by the wickedness of men on earth, and said he would get rid of the men and the animals by sending a flood of water.

There was a good man called Noah living with his sons Shem, Ham and Japheth. God told him to build himself an ark and take his family onto it, with two of every kind of animal, bird and reptile. Noah must take a store of food, so that when the flood came, his family and the animals would be safe. The flood covered the earth and after a long time Noah sent a dove to see if the waters had begun to go down. The dove returned with an olive twig, and when Noah looked out of the ark he could see dry land on the mountains.

Noah and his sons came out of the ark and God blessed them and told them to take their families and to rule the earth.

```
J K R A E V O D G
F A R E T A W I A
L S P M A H W F N
O H G H Z T N A I
O E O X E B O M M
D M D V Y T A I A
C B I R D K H L L
R L H T R A E Y T
O S E L I T P E R
```

### Solution

GOD
EARTH
FLOOD
WATER
NOAH
SHEM
HAM
JAPHETH
ARK
ANIMAL
BIRD
REPTILE
FAMILY
DOVE
OLIVE TWIG

```
J K R A E V O D G
F A R E T A W I A
L S P M A H W F N
O H G H Z T N A I
O E O X E B O M M
D M D V Y T A I A
C B I R D K H L L
R L H T R A E Y T
O S E L I T P E R
```

For instructions for Word Maze puzzles see page 2 of *Hands*.

### FIRE AND WATER

WHICH FIRE IS:

1.   FIRE – – – – – – –   – a place where fire engines are kept
2.   FIRE – – – – –   – apparatus for giving warning of fire
3.   FIRE – – – – – –   – a machine for putting fires out
4.   FIRE – – – – –   – a juggler who seems to eat fire

### WHAT KIND OF WORD

#### Solution

1. FIRE-STATION
2. FIRE ALARM
3. FIRE ENGINE
4. FIRE EATER

PUZZLES

FLOAT SOME DEAD MATCHES ON CLEAN WATER IN A CIRCLE LIKE THIS →

* Touch the middle of the water with SOAP, and the matches move apart

What came upon the apostles.....

① 1st letter of
② 3rd letter of
③ 4th letter of
④ 3rd letter of .....
⑤ 1st letter of
⑥ 2nd letter of
⑦ 3rd letter of
⑧ 2nd letter of ........
⑨ 2nd letter of
⑩ 8th letter of

at Pentecost?

(Holy Spirit)

# Storms at Sea!

1. Who was shipwrecked near Malta? (Acts 27:13-44)

   _ _ _ _

2. Who calmed a storm at Galilee? (Matthew 8:23-27)

   _ _ _ _ _

3. Who drifted on the stormy waters for 150 days? (Genesis 7:23-24)

   _ _ _ _

**Answers:** 1. Paul  2. Jesus  3. Noah

# Naaman's visit to Elisha

READ THE STORY IN 2 KINGS 5:1-14

START

NAAMAN lived in S_ _ _ _

His wife came from I_ _ _ _ _

Naaman was ill... he was a L_ _ _ _

So he set off to visit E_ _ _ _ _

...with talents _ _ of SILVER...

...and shekels _ of GOLD...

...and a _ _ _ _ _

...and _ festal garments!

The King of Israel was so scared, he tore his _ _ _ _ _

Elisha told him to wash _ _ _ _ _ times in the Jordan river

That made Naaman really A_ _ _ _!

He was calmed down by his S_ _ _ _ _ _ _

...and bathed _ _ _ _ _ times in the _ _ _ _ _ _

...and sure enough, Naaman was made well again!

**Answers:** Naaman lived in Syria. His wife came from Israel. Naaman was a leper. He set off to visit Elisha with ten talents of silver and 6,000 shekels of gold, and a letter, and ten festal garments. The King of Israel . . . tore his robes. Elisha told him to wash seven times in the Jordan River. That made Naaman really angry! He was calmed down by his servants, and bathed seven times in the River Jordan.

## ~ The Christian Family ~

- First trace round yourself or someone else on a large piece of paper — or several joined together. Cut out and fix to the wall with blue tak.
- Take a sheet of paper 21 x 29½ cm and fold in half

 and again into 3

- Place the girl or the boy shape over the front and cut round it. One piece of paper makes 6 shapes. On each shape write a way in which one person serves others, i.e. "nurse", "teacher", "mother", "father", "busdriver", etc. . . and stick them all over the large "body".

COLOUR IT IN!

## ~ Jesus in the Temple ~

Luke 2:41-50

Can you help Joseph and Mary to find their son?

## Joseph and the Multi-coloured Coat

**Across:**

1. How old was Joseph when his father gave him a multi-coloured coat?
2. Which brother did not want to kill Joseph?
3. His brothers threw Joseph into a dry one.
4. When he heard of Joseph's "death", Jacob did this for many days.

**Down:**

1. Joseph's first dream was about these.
5. How many stars bowed down to Joseph in his second dream?
6. Where were the Ishmaelites going?
7. Joseph's brother dipped his tunic into a goat's – – – – –.
8. Joseph was sold as one of these.

(Answers in Genesis 37:2-36)

### Solution

| Across | Down |
|--------|------|
| 1. Seventeen | 1. Sheaves |
| 2. Reuben | 5. Eleven |
| 3. Well | 6. Egypt |
| 4. Mourned | 7. Blood |
| | 8. Slave |

# A Friend is someone . . .

... who shares.

... who helps you out.

... who makes you feel good.

... who comforts

... who says *nice* things about you when you're not around.

... who forgives.

# THE SHEEP FAMILY
## GAME

For 2 or more players. You will need a dice and a counter for each player.

Place counters on start. Players throw the dice in turn. A player may only land on a member of the Sheep Family. If a number leads him or her to a monster, he/she must remain in the same space until the next go. The first player to reach the fold is the WINNER!

The Good Samaritan    (Luke 10:29-37)

## FAMILY        WORD MAZE

The Story of Ruth.   (From the Book of Ruth)

During a time of famine in the land of Judah, a man from Bethlehem took his wife Naomi and his two sons to live in the neighbouring country of Moab. They settled down there and one of his sons married a Moabite woman called Ruth and the other son's wife was called Orpah.

After a time Naomi's husband and their two sons died and she was very sad and decided to return to Bethlehem. Her two daughters-in-law travelled with her towards Judah, but she thought they would be unhappy in a strange land and begged them to return to Moab. But Ruth said "Don't urge me to leave you or to turn back from you. Where you go, I will go, and where you stay, I will stay. Your people will be my people and your God my God."

So Naomi and Ruth returned to Bethlehem together, and Ruth married a relative of Naomi's called Boaz. They had a son who was to be the grandfather of King David.

For instructions on how to make a badge see page 5 of *Light & Darkness.*

~ Badge to make ~

```
G D N A B S U H M
O B E E L P O E P
D H G F C D H D N
O A N I F E I B A
R D A W L V A O O
P U R H A O G A M
A J T D M H J Z I
H E S H S N O S K
B E V I T A L E R
```

**Solution**

JUDAH        HUSBAND
BETHLEHEM    STRANGE
WIFE         PEOPLE
NAOMI        GOD
SONS         RELATIVE
MOAB         BOAZ
RUTH         DAVID
ORPAH

For instructions for Word Maze puzzles see page 2 of *Hands.*

What is Jesus asking of his friends ?

(Read John 15:14)

(**Answers:** You are my friends if you do what I command you.)

# FAMILY AND FRIENDS 4

## NAME THE SAINT

– who was the sister of Lazarus, and who welcomed Jesus into her home?

On what day do we especially remember her?

Read about her in Luke 10:38-41 and John chs. 11 and 12.

> St Martha
> 29th July

## FAMILY  WHAT KIND OF WORD

WHICH FATHER IS:

1. FATHER— —
2. FATHER— — — — — — —
3. FATHER / — / — — —
4. FATHER'S — — —

– behaving like a father
– Santa Claus
– the father of one's husband or wife
– a day in June when fathers are honoured

### Solution

1. FATHERLY
2. FATHER CHRISTMAS
3. FATHER-IN-LAW
4. FATHER'S DAY

## ~ Make a Family & Friends File ~

**You will need:**
- A small empty box (i.e. a shoebox)
- Scissors
- Thin card
- Felt-tip pens.

1. Cut round the box to make a holder around 7 cm deep.
2. Measure the width of your box, and cut cards to fit.
3. Make cards for family and friends as shown. You can either draw their pictures or use photographs which they can spare.
4. You can add your own headings, too, and write things on the backs of the cards.

NAME :
ADDRESS :

TELEPHONE :
BIRTHDAY :        HAIR :

COLOUR OF EYES :
FINGERPRINTS :

PETS :
FAVOURITE HOBBY :
FAVOURITE FOOD :
FAVOURITE COLOUR :

## ~ Name the Twelve Apostles ~

Unjumble the name of each Apostle:

1. PREET
2. MAJES
3. HONJ
4. WREAND
5. HIPPIL
6. WEBROTHAMLO
7. AWTHMET
8. MOTASH
9. SMEAJ
10. DUTHSEAD
11. NOIMS
12. SUDJA

You can check your answers by reading Mark 3:13-19

1. _____
2. _____
3. _____
4. _____
5. _____
6. _____
7. _____
8. _____
9. _____
10. _____
11. _____
12. _____

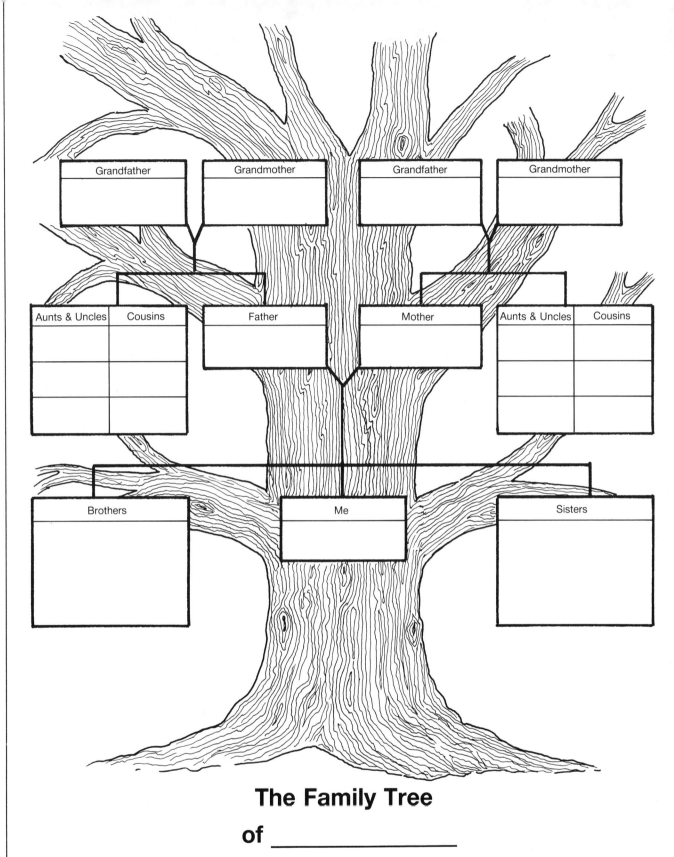

| Grandfather | Grandmother | | Grandfather | Grandmother |
| --- | --- | --- | --- | --- |

| Aunts & Uncles | Cousins | Father | | Mother | Aunts & Uncles | Cousins |
| --- | --- | --- | --- | --- | --- | --- |

| Brothers | Me | Sisters |
| --- | --- | --- |

# The Family Tree

## of _____

## FAMILY          WORD CIRCLE

How many words of three letters or more can you make from the letters in the circle? When you have found as many as you can, try and make one word of seven letters using all the letters.

This word means some very important members of the family.

| | | | |
| --- | --- | --- | --- |
| CHIDE | DINE | HID | LINE |
| CHILD | DIRE | HIDE | NICE |
| CHIN | END | HIRE | RED |
| CINDER | HEIR | IRE | RICE |
| CRIED | HEN | LICE | RICH |
| DEN | HER | LIED | RID |
| DIN | HERD | LID | RIND          CHILDREN |

Word circle letters: C, R, E, I, H, D, L, N

# HANDS 1

## BLESSING HANDS

COLOUR THE PICTURE OF JACOB BEING
BLESSED BY ISAAC (GENESIS 27)

What gifts did
the wise men
offer Jesus?

NIRF K ACN ESE

OLGD

RYMH

Fi(nger)prints

clean paper

news paper

ink pad

① Collect as many as you can

② Examine them carefully....
EVERYONE IS DIFFERENT!

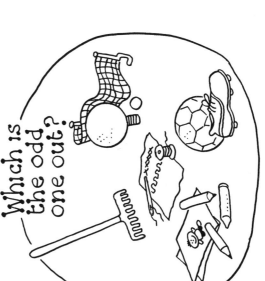

Which is
the odd
one out?

(Answer: Football – all the others need hands.)

**Jokes**

Q. Why was the left hand sad?
A. Because he never did anything right!

Q. Why is a banana like a horse?
A. They're both measured in hands.

Q. Why are your hands like desert islands?
A. They both have palms!

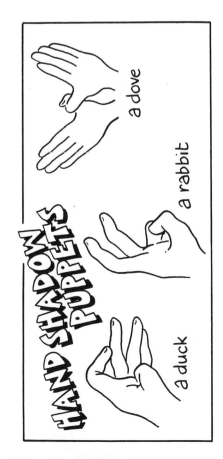

# HANDS

# WORD MAZE

The Widow of Nain   (Luke 7:11-15)

Jesus and his disciples went to a town called Nain. When they got there a dead person was being carried out – it was the only son of his mother who was a widow. When Jesus saw her, his heart went out to her and he said "Don't cry."

Then he touched the coffin with his hand and said "Young man, I say to you, get up." The dead man sat up and began to talk, and Jesus gave him back to his mother. All the people there were filled with amazement and praised God.

| T | D | E | S | I | A | R | P | T |
|---|---|---|---|---|---|---|---|---|
| O | E | L | P | O | E | P | N | M |
| U | A | S | S | U | S | E | J | O |
| C | B | O | H | C | M | D | E | T |
| H | F | N | D | E | A | D | G | H |
| E | H | J | Z | N | A | I | N | E |
| D | K | A | L | M | N | R | O | R |
| P | M | Q | N | K | L | A | T | S |
| A | T | W | O | D | I | W | U | V |

**Solution**

JESUS
NAIN
DEAD
SON
MOTHER
WIDOW
HEART
TOUCHED
HAND
TALK
PEOPLE
AMAZEMENT
PRAISED

| T | D | E | S | I | A | R | P | T |
|---|---|---|---|---|---|---|---|---|
| O | E | L | P | O | E | P | N | M |
| U | A | S | S | U | S | E | J | O |
| C | B | O | H | C | M | D | E | T |
| H | F | N | D | E | A | D | G | H |
| E | H | J | Z | N | A | I | N | E |
| D | K | A | L | M | N | R | O | R |
| P | M | Q | N | K | L | A | T | S |
| A | T | W | O | D | I | W | U | V |

## Instructions for Word Maze puzzles

When you read the story you will see that some of the words are underlined. Look for these words in the grid. The words read forward, backwards, up, down and diagonally – always in a straight line. Cross through each word as you find it. Some words in the grid overlap, so the letters may be used more than once. You won't need to use all the letters in the grid.

'An eye for an eye, a tooth for a tooth'... That's fair

...BUT WHO WINS?

Take 1st letter of NORMAN
Take 3rd letter of GEORGE
Take 3rd letter of ROBERT
Take 2nd letter of JOHN
Take 5th letter of AMANDA
Take 5th letter of HARRY

( _ _ _ _ _ _ )

draw round your hand, to make a PRAYER CARD

Loving Father, use my hands

HAND SHADOW PUPPETS

a dove

a rabbit

a duck

# HEALING HANDS

### ACROSS

② MARK 1: 29-31
The name of the woman's son-in-law

③ LUKE 8: 40-56
The name of the girl's father

④ LUKE 7: 11-17
The town where the widow lived

### DOWN

① MATTHEW 19: 13-15
The disciples wanted to turn them away

**Solution:** 1. Children  2. Simon  3. Jairus  4. Nain

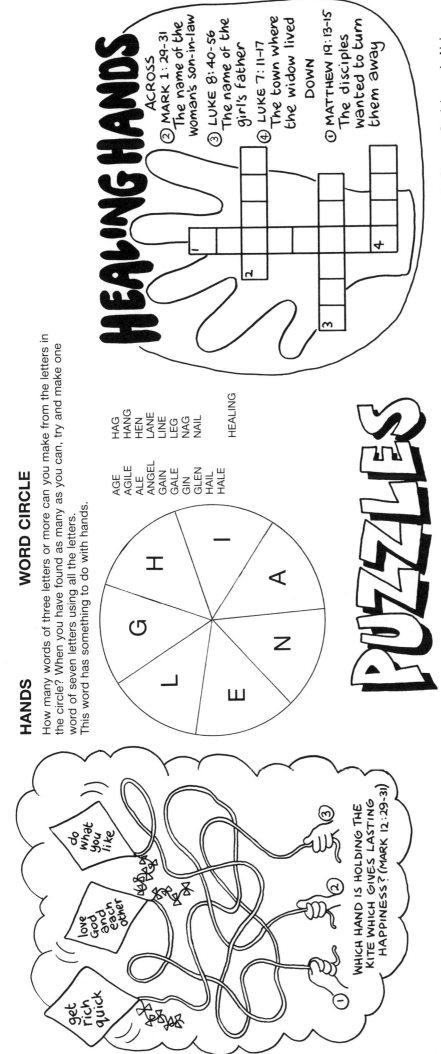

## HANDS

## WORD CIRCLE

How many words of three letters or more can you make from the letters in the circle? When you have found as many as you can, try and make one word of seven letters using all the letters. This word has something to do with hands.

L G H I A N E

AGE
AGILE
ALE
ANGEL
GAIN
GALE
GIN
GLEN
HAIL
HALE

HAG
HANG
HEN
LANE
LINE
LEG
NAG
NAIL

HEALING

# PUZZLES

do what you like

love God and each other

get rich quick

③
②
①

WHICH HAND IS HOLDING THE KITE WHICH GIVES LASTING HAPPINESS? (MARK 12:29-31)

## HOW CAN WE BEST LIVE OUR LIVES?...

COLOUR IN THE DOTTED SPACES TO SEE WHAT JESUS SAID (JOHN 15:12)

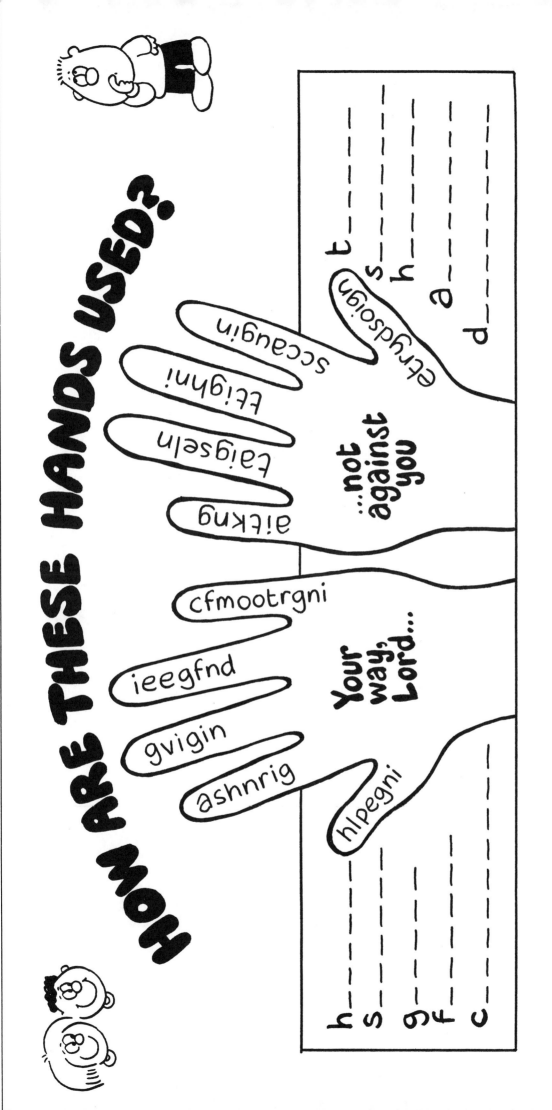

# HOW ARE THESE HANDS USED?

sccaugin

ffighni

faigseln

aitkng

...not against you

cfmootrgni

ieegfnd

gvigin

ashnrig

Your way, Lord...

hlpegni

etrygdsoign

t
s
h
a
d

h
s
g
F
c

# PUZZLES

## what HAND is...

good for blowing your nose

useful

good looking

something to hold on to

as much as a hand can hold

| | | | | | | | | | |
|---|---|---|---|---|---|---|---|---|---|
| H | A | N | D | | | | | | |
| H | A | N | D | | | | | | |
| H | A | N | D | | | | | | |
| H | A | N | D | | | | | | |
| H | A | N | D | | | | | | |

**Solution:** Handkerchief, Hands, Handsome, Handle, Handful.

Join the dots
to finish
the picture

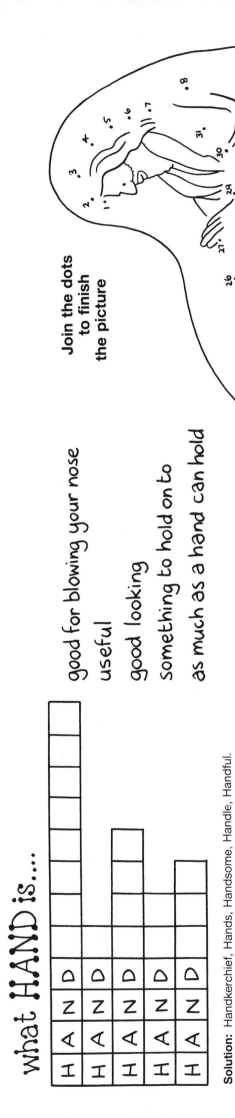

**JESUS HEALS A MAN**

(Read Matthew 8:1-4, or Mark 1:40-45, or Luke 5:12-16)

1. Eternal life.   2. Rest.
3. The Kingdom/Riches in heaven.

PRESENTS!

FOR YOU

FOR YOU

FOR YOU

JOHN 4:7-14     MATTHEW 11:28-30     LUKE 12:32-34

What presents does God give us? Look them up to see

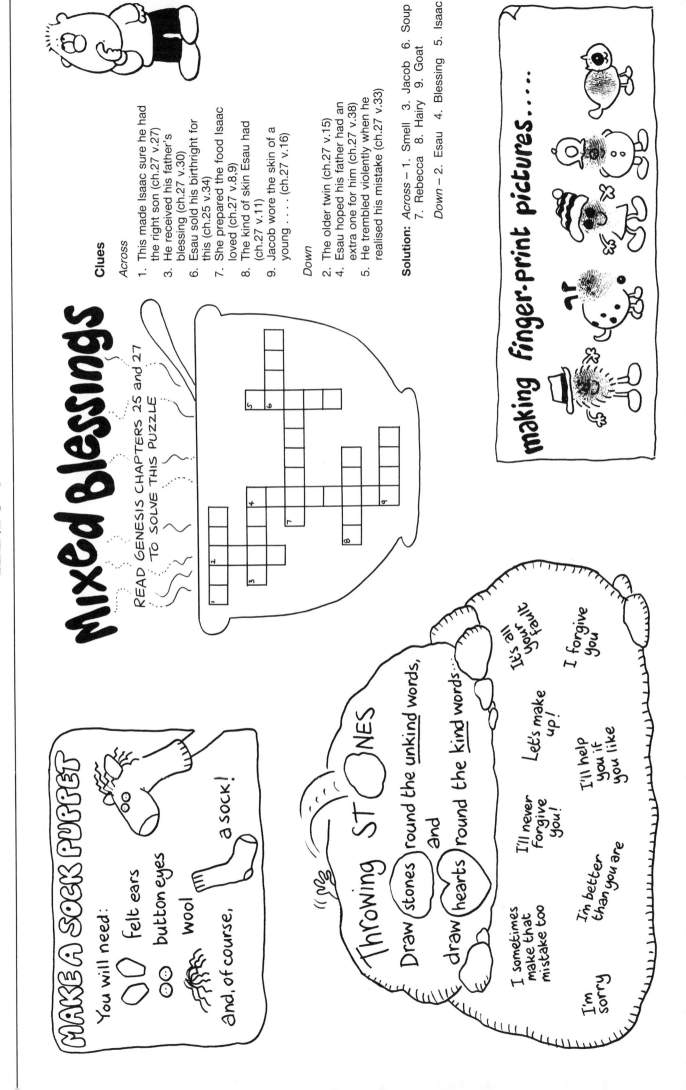

# Mixed Blessings

READ GENESIS CHAPTERS 25 and 27 TO SOLVE THIS PUZZLE

## Clues

### Across

1. This made Isaac sure he had the right son (ch.27 v.27)
3. He received his father's blessing (ch.27 v.30)
6. Esau sold his birthright for this (ch.25 v.34)
7. She prepared the food Isaac loved (ch.27 v.8,9)
8. The kind of skin Esau had (ch.27 v.11)
9. Jacob wore the skin of a young . . . . (ch.27 v.16)

### Down

2. The older twin (ch.27 v.15)
4. Esau hoped his father had an extra one for him (ch.27 v.38)
5. He trembled violently when he realised his mistake (ch.27 v.33)

**Solution:** *Across* – 1. Smell  3. Jacob  6. Soup  7. Rebecca  8. Hairy  9. Goat
*Down* – 2. Esau  4. Blessing  5. Isaac

## making finger-print pictures.....

## MAKE A SOCK PUPPET

You will need:

◇ felt ears
◉◉ button eyes
🌀 wool

And, of course, a sock!

## Throwing ST⚫NES

Draw (stones) round the <u>unkind</u> words,
and
draw (hearts) round the <u>kind</u> words....

It's all your fault
I'll never forgive you!
Let's make up!
I forgive you
I'll help you if you like
I sometimes make that mistake too
I'm better than you are
I'm sorry

# ~ Make a Magnetic Beetle ~

**You will need:**

1. A shoe box lid or similar
2. A paper cup
3. Scissors
4. Sellotape
5. A small piece of plasticine or self-hardening clay (about 2 cm diam.)
6. A small nut or bolt, or short screw
7. A magnet
8. Felt-tip pens

- Turn lid upside down.
- Cut a "doorway" in the rim of the cup. Turn it upside-down and tape it into one corner of the lid.
- Draw a winding narrow path to the paper cup
- Decorate the way with flowers etc.
- Make a beetle with the plasticine or clay. Stick the metal piece into the base.
- With the beetle at the start of the path and holding the magnet beneath the lid, lead the beetle along the path to his home!

## ~ Badge to make ~

To make this badge you will need:

* a piece of card (you can cut it off an empty cereal box)
* scissors
* glue
* a small safety pin
* sellotape
* felt-tips

1. Colour the badge.
2. Cut it out and glue it onto card.
3. Cut round the badge
4. Sellotape the safety pin onto back.

Note:
The badges can be covered with self-adhesive plastic.

## Which road leads to LIFE ?

Read Matthew 7:13-14

THIS WAY  THIS WAY

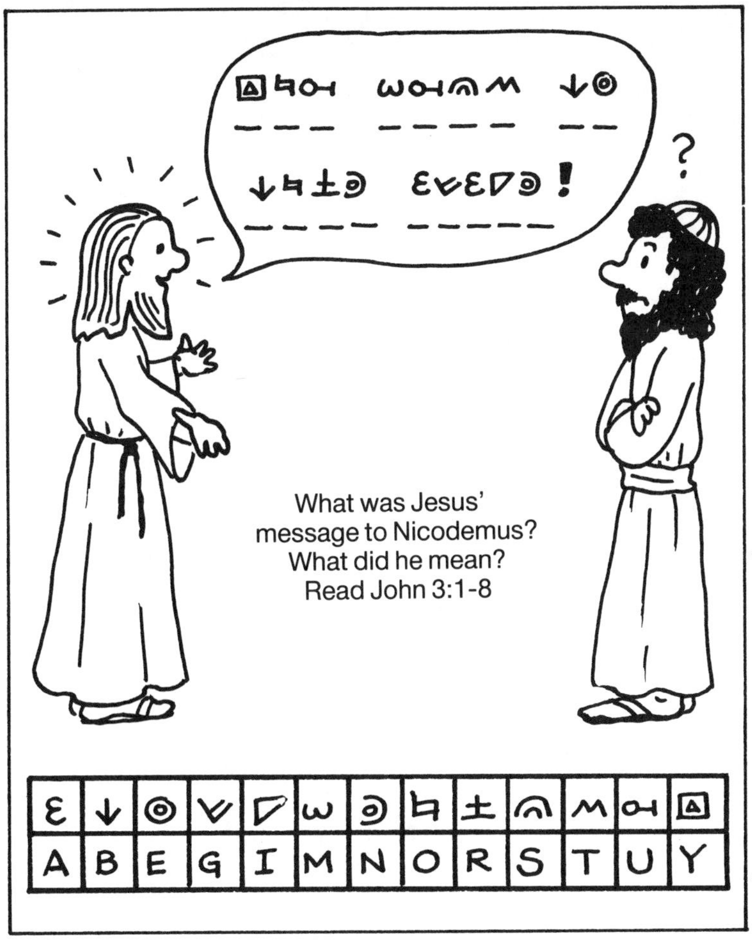


What was Jesus' message to Nicodemus? What did he mean? Read John 3:1-8

(**Answer:** You must be born again.)

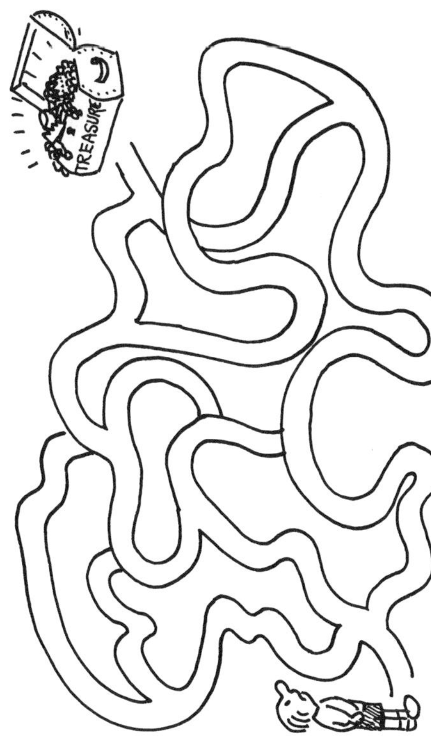


Help Arthur to find the way to the treasure.

## THE WAY

WHICH CHRIST IS

## WHAT KIND OF WORD

1. CHRIST-- –to baptize
2. CHRIST---- –those who follow Jesus
3. CHRIST--- –the season that celebrates the birth of Jesus

**Solution**

1. CHRISTEN
2. CHRISTIANS
3. CHRISTMAS

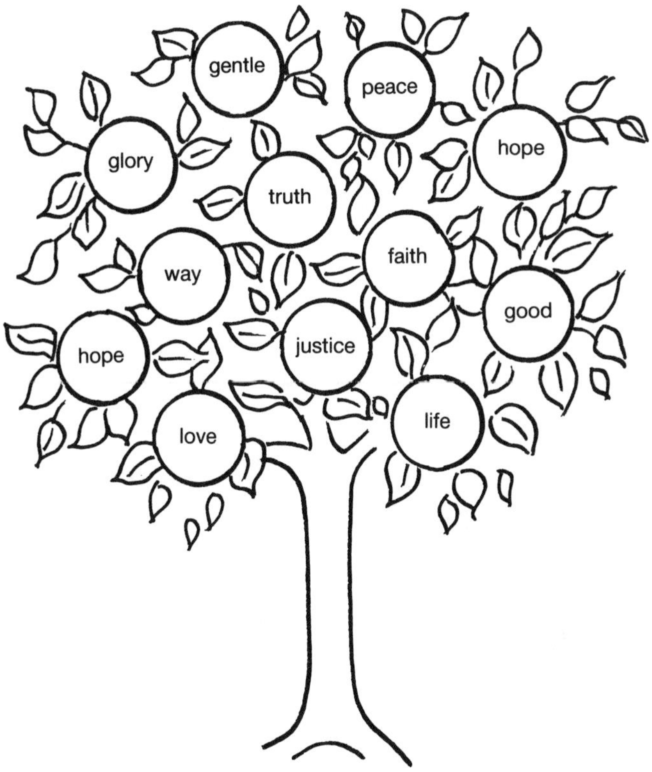


## JESUS SAID:

"I am the________, the________ and the ________."

Read John 14:6 to help you pick the right words from the Word Tree.

## ~ Help Jenny to pack ~

Jenny is going on a spiritual journey with Jesus. Help her to pack what she needs.

trust, joy, colouring books
shoes, strength, sweets
wisdom, perseverance, generosity
love, toys, kindness
courage, inner peace, toothbrush
forgiveness, teddy bear, trainers
felt tips, compass

Can you think of anything else?

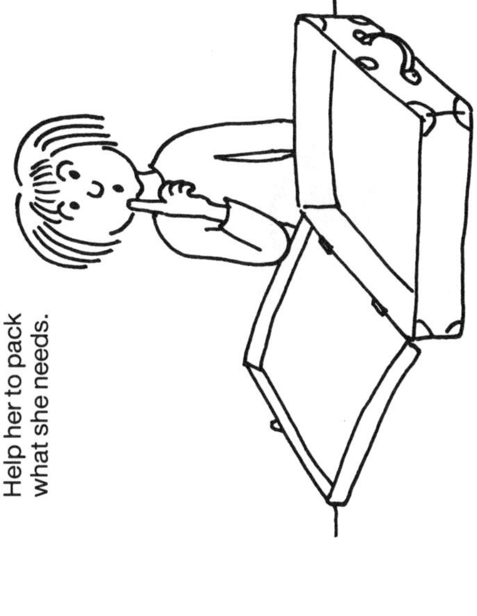

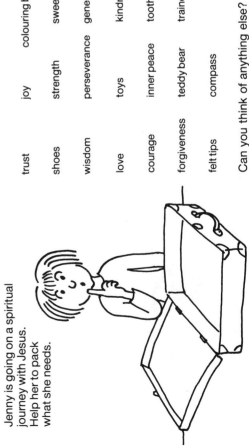

# THE 10 COMMANDMENTS

EXODUS 20:1-17

DEUTERONOMY 5:1-21

1 WORSHIP NO _ _ _ EXCEPT ME.

2 DO NOT BOW DOWN TO ANY _ _ _ _ _ OR _ _ _ _ _ _ _ _ IT.

3 DO NOT _ _ _ _ _ _ _ MY NAME.

4 KEEP THE SABBATH HOLY~ THE SEVENTH DAY IS A DAY OF _ _ _ _ DEDICATED TO ME.

5 RESPECT YOUR _ _ _ _ _ _ _ AND YOUR _ _ _ _ _ _ _

6 DO NOT KILL.

7 BE FAITHFUL TO YOUR HUSBAND OR WIFE.

8 DO NOT STEAL.

9 DO NOT ACCUSE ANYONE FALSELY.

10 DO NOT ENVY WHAT OTHER PEOPLE OWN.

## ~ Make a Coin Headdress ~

Remember the woman who lost a coin from her headdress, and wouldn't rest until she found it? (Luke 15:8-10)

**You will need:**
- thin card
- scissors
- a 5p coin
- gold or silver paint *or* sweet papers and bits of foil
- a length of string or narrow ribbon to tie round your head
- a bodkin

1. Trace around the 5p coin to make as many coins as you want.
2. Cut them out.
3. Paint or spray them, or cover them in foil.
4. Thread through the centre of each with the bodkin and string or ribbon.

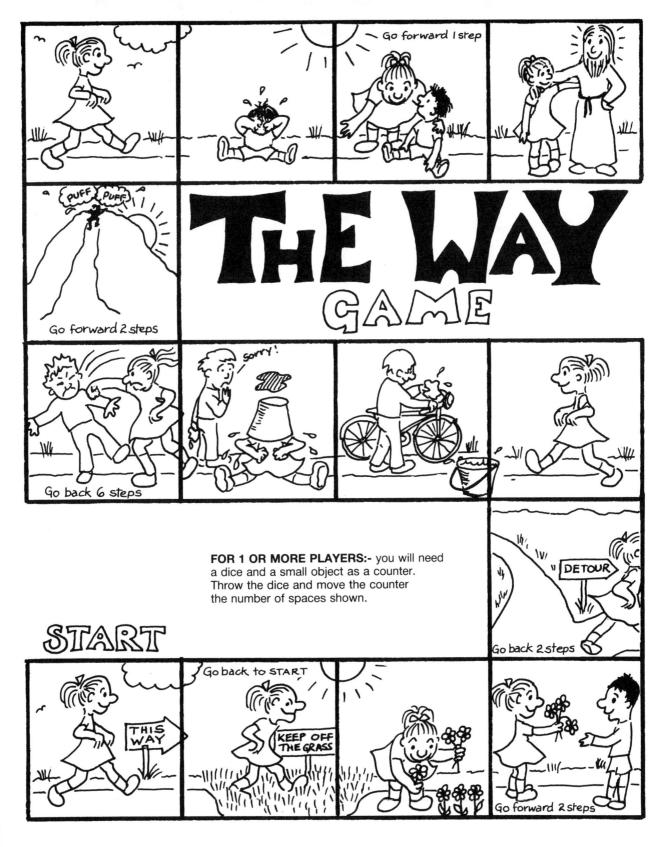

**FOR 1 OR MORE PLAYERS:-** you will need a dice and a small object as a counter. Throw the dice and move the counter the number of spaces shown.

## THE WAY    WORD CIRCLE

How many words of three letters or more can you make from the letters in the circle? No proper names can be used and no plurals. When you have found as many words as you can, try and make one word of eight letters using all the letters.

This word means a follower of Jesus.

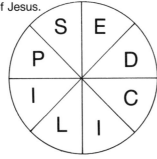

| | |
|---|---|
| CLIP | PILE |
| DICE | SIDE |
| DIE | SIP |
| IDLE | SLED |
| LED | SLICE |
| LID | SLID |
| LICE | SLIDE |
| LIE | SPED |
| LIED | SPIED |
| LIP | |
| LISP | DISCIPLE |
| PIE | |
| PIED | |

## ~ Make a Serpent ~

**You will need:**

- scissors
- felt tips
- sellotape
- a piece of thread

1. Colour the serpent.
2. Cut round the heavy lines.
3. Sellotape one end of the thread from the serpent's head.
4. Dangle it in front of your friends.

# ~SIGNS~

STOP

TURN RIGHT

GO

SNACKS

DANGER

SLOW DOWN

COWS CROSSING

On a journey, there are always signs to guide you on your way. Look at these in the mirror to see what they say!

Can you think of some signs to help someone on a spiritual journey?

## WORD MAZE

For instructions for Word Maze puzzles see page 2 of *Hands*.

### THE WAY
Mark 12:28-31

One of the teachers of the law asked Jesus "Which is the most important of all the commandments?"

"The most important" answered Jesus "is this . . . Love the Lord your God with all your heart and with all your soul and with all your mind and with all your strength. The second it this. Love your neighbour as yourself. There is no commandment greater than these."

### Solution

TEACHERS
LAW
JESUS
IMPORTANT
LOVE
LORD
GOD
HEART
SOUL
MIND
STRENGTH
NEIGHBOUR
GREATER

| R | U | O | B | H | G | I | E | N |
|---|---|---|---|---|---|---|---|---|
| H | T | G | N | E | R | T | S | A |
| L | B | L | W | J | D | R | E | M |
| O | S | O | A | G | E | D | H | I |
| V | O | R | L | H | O | S | K | N |
| E | U | D | C | G | L | H | U | D |
| N | L | A | T | R | A | E | H | S |
| R | E | T | A | E | R | G | R | T |
| T | N | A | T | R | O | P | M | I |

## SERMON on the MOUNT ~ CROSSWORD ~

Matthew 5:1-12

### Across
1. These sayings are called the B _ _ _ _ _ _ _ _
2. What will the gentle inherit?
3. The pure in _ _ _ _ _ shall see God.

### Down
4. Who shall be recognised as the Children of God?
5. Blessed are those who hunger and _ _ _ _ _ _ .
6. What do the poor in spirit and the persecuted have in common?
7. Those who _ _ _ _ _ will be comforted.
8. Who will be shown mercy?

### Solution

*Across*
1. Beatitudes
2. Earth
3. Heart

*Down*
4. Peacemakers
5. Thirst
6. Heaven
7. Mourn
8. Merciful

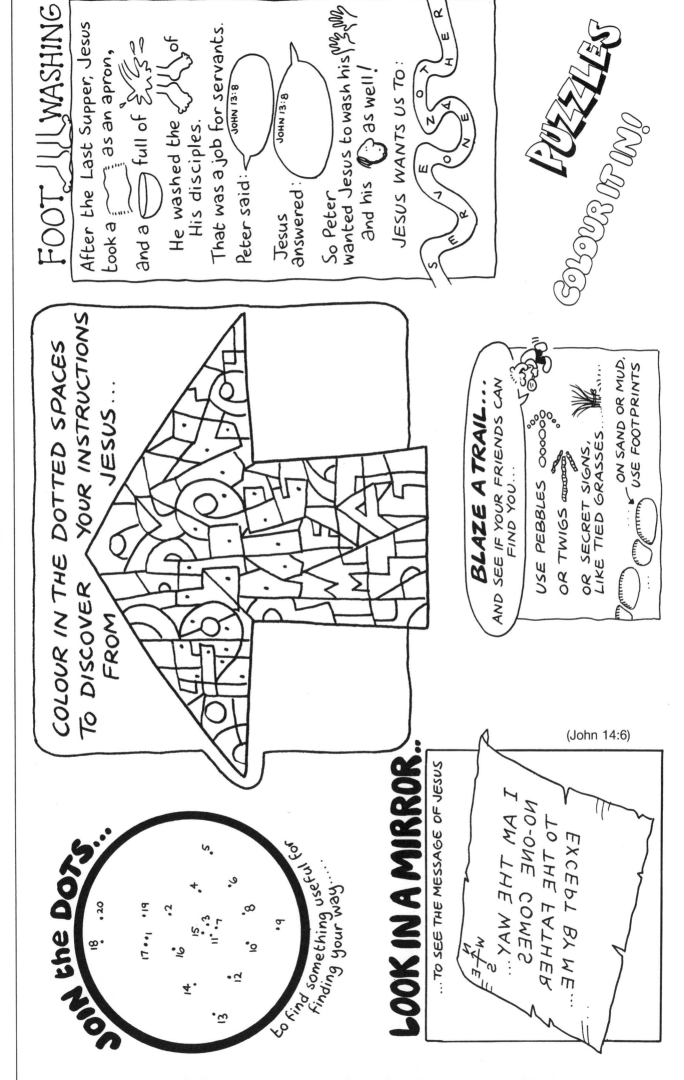

## Make a plaster cast of animal prints in mud....

YOU WILL NEED :-

- A STRIP OF CARD
- PAPER CLIPS
- PLASTER
- WATER

and... SOME PRINTS IN MUD OR SAND

① CURL THE CARD ROUND THE PRINT, AND FIX WITH CLIPS...

② MIX THE PLASTER

③ POUR INTO THE PRINT AND LEAVE TO SET

## Why did Peter start sinking?

Look up in MATTHEW 14 v. 30....
Because _____

_____

_____

## FEET

Jesus walking on the water

### WORD MAZE

(Mark 6:45-52)

When they got to the lake Jesus told his disciples to go on ahead of him in the boat. He left them and went into the hills to pray until evening. By that time the boat was in the middle of the lake and Jesus was alone on the land. He saw the disciples straining at the oars because the wind was against them. When night came he went to them, walking on the lake and as soon as they saw him they were terrified. Immediately he spoke to them and said "Take courage. It is I. Don't be afraid." Then he climbed into the boat with them, and the wind died down.

```
Q E G A R U O C D
D I A R F A H E W
N O C Y X J I T A
I A A L E F L H L
W R P S I A L G K
P S U R K M S I I
J S R E K L B N N
M E S T A O B E G
T G N I N E V E D
```

### Solution

LAKE
JESUS
BOAT
HILLS
PRAY
EVENING
OARS
WIND
NIGHT
WALKING
TERRIFIED
COURAGE
AFRAID
CLIMBED

```
Q E G A R U O C D
D I A R F A H E W
N O C Y X J I T A
I A A L E F L H L
W R P S I A L G K
P S U R K M S I I
J S R E K L B N N
M E S T A O B E G
T G N I N E V E D
```

For instructions for Word Maze puzzles see page 2 of *Hands*.

[This puzzle should be with the **Fire and Water** theme but there was no space for it!]

## WHAT a CATCH!

TO SOLVE THIS PUZZLE, READ LUKE 5: 1-11

### ACROSS

3 How many boats on the beach?

4 They caught so many fish that their nets began to _____

5 See 2 DOWN

### DOWN

1 What was Simon's other name?

2 (and 5 Across) What had the fishermen done without success?

### Solution

*Across* – 3. Two  4. Break  5. Hard
*Down* – 1. Peter  2. Worked

**FEET 3**

(Read the story in Genesis 11:27 . . .)

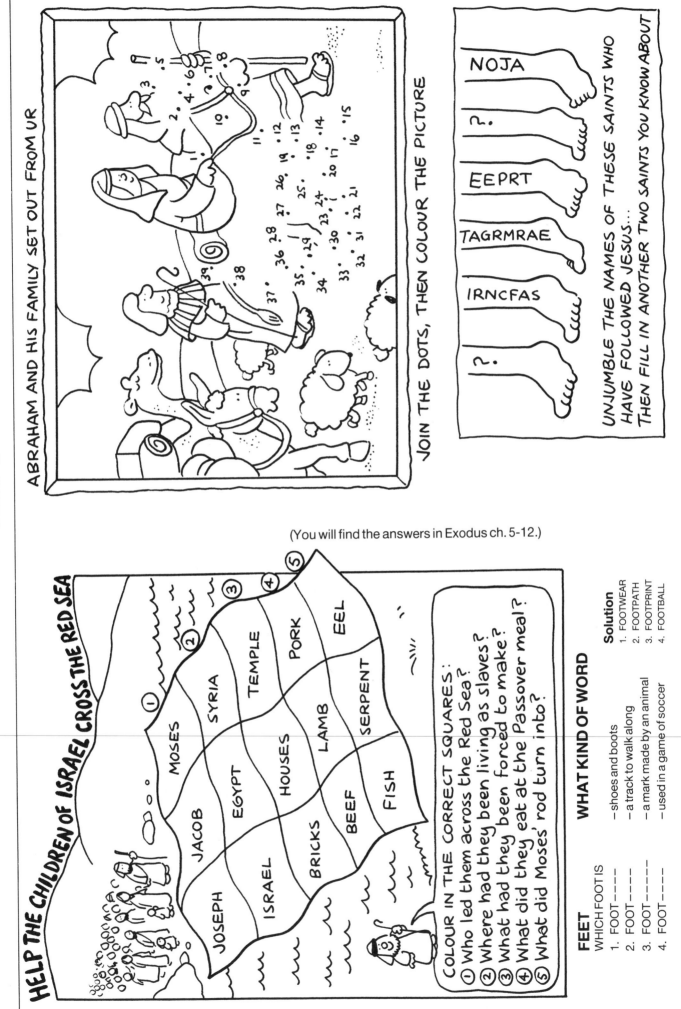

ABRAHAM AND HIS FAMILY SET OUT FROM UR

JOIN THE DOTS, THEN COLOUR THE PICTURE

NOJA

?.

EEPRT

TAGRMRAE

IRNCFAS

?.

UNJUMBLE THE NAMES OF THESE SAINTS WHO HAVE FOLLOWED JESUS...
THEN FILL IN ANOTHER TWO SAINTS YOU KNOW ABOUT

HELP THE CHILDREN OF ISRAEL CROSS THE RED SEA

(You will find the answers in Exodus ch. 5-12.)

JOSEPH — ISRAEL — JACOB — MOSES
EGYPT — SYRIA — TEMPLE
BRICKS — HOUSES — LAMB — PORK — EEL
BEEF — SERPENT
FISH

COLOUR IN THE CORRECT SQUARES:
① Who led them across the Red Sea?
② Where had they been living as slaves?
③ What had they been forced to make?
④ What did they eat at the Passover meal?
⑤ What did Moses' rod turn into?

**FEET**
WHICH FOOT IS
1. FOOT – – – –
2. FOOT – – – –
3. FOOT – – – – –
4. FOOT – – – – –

**WHAT KIND OF WORD**
– shoes and boots
– a track to walk along
– a mark made by an animal
– used in a game of soccer

**Solution**
1. FOOTWEAR
2. FOOTPATH
3. FOOTPRINT
4. FOOTBALL

# FIND THE TREASURE!

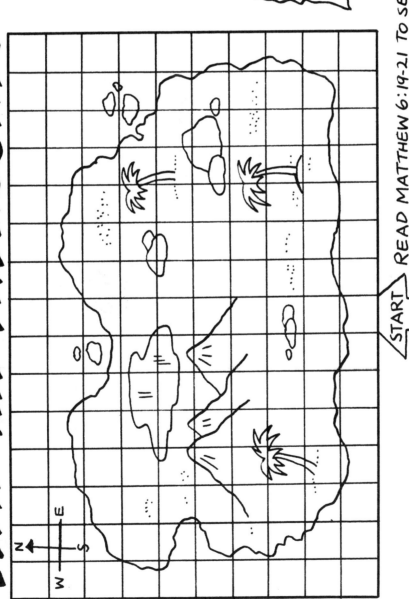

## Directions:-

Sail
1 square North
7 squares East
2 squares North, then land
3 squares West
2 squares North West
1 square North
1 square North West
2 squares West
1 square South West
1 square North West

### Here lies the treasure!

START READ MATTHEW 6:19-21 TO SEE WHAT JESUS SAYS ABOUT TREASURE

PUZZLES

Colour it in!

PUZZLES

Colour it in!

# JESUS heals a paralysed man....

(READ THE STORY IN LUKE 5:17-26)

...but he didn't just heal him so he could walk again, did he?
Use the code to discover the other way the man was healed....

# WHICH TRACKS LEAD TO THE SHEEP FOLD?

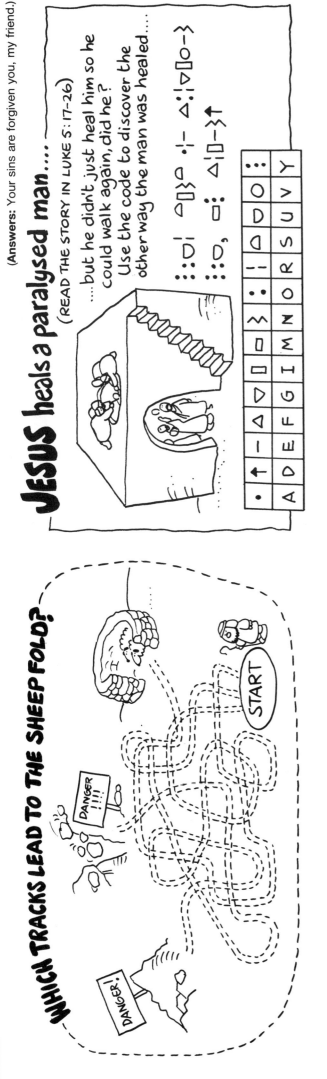

DANGER!!!!

DANGER!!!!

START

# stepping stones

fear

despair

bitterness

worry

Take the first letter of each picture to find out what helps us walk safely and boldly through life.

(Answer: Faith)

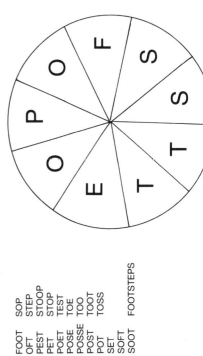

## FEET    WORD CIRCLE

How many words of three letters or more can you make from the letters in the circle? No proper names can be used and no plurals. When you have found as many words as you can, try and make one word of nine letters using all the letters.
This word has something to do with feet.

FOOT
OFT
PEST
PET
POET
POSE
POSSE
POST
POT
SET
SOFT
SOOT

SOP
STEP
STOOP
STOP
TEST
TOE
TOO
TOOT
TOSS

FOOTSTEPS